Ruth Heller's
Designs for Coloring

SNOWFLAKES

Publishers · GROSSET & DUNLAP · New York

Ruth Heller's DESIGNS FOR COLORING offer a stimulating
and exciting visual adventure. Each title in the series provides an
endless variety of fascinating possibilities for exploring forms,
shapes, patterns, and colors. You can work in a realistic, graphic,
or decorative style, combining colors in all sorts of ingenious
ways. Or you may find pleasure in repeating the patterns in a
more symmetrical, abstract style.

Just as no two people are exactly alike, no two people will see
exactly the same possibilities when coloring these varied objects,
designs, and patterns. You are free to go wherever your imagina-
tion directs you. Whatever the direction you choose to explore,
the results will be satisfying and fulfilling. These are books
guaranteed to furnish many hours of creative pleasure for
people of all ages.

Created by award-winning artist/designer Ruth Heller,
DESIGNS FOR COLORING are unique among coloring books.
The high-quality paper is suitable for use with crayons, felt-tipped
pens, water paints, pencils, or pastels. You can use bold, bright
colors or lighter, subtler shades. You may even want to frame
an especially pleasing page—or transfer a pattern to a piece of
embroidery, needlepoint, pottery, or mosaic.

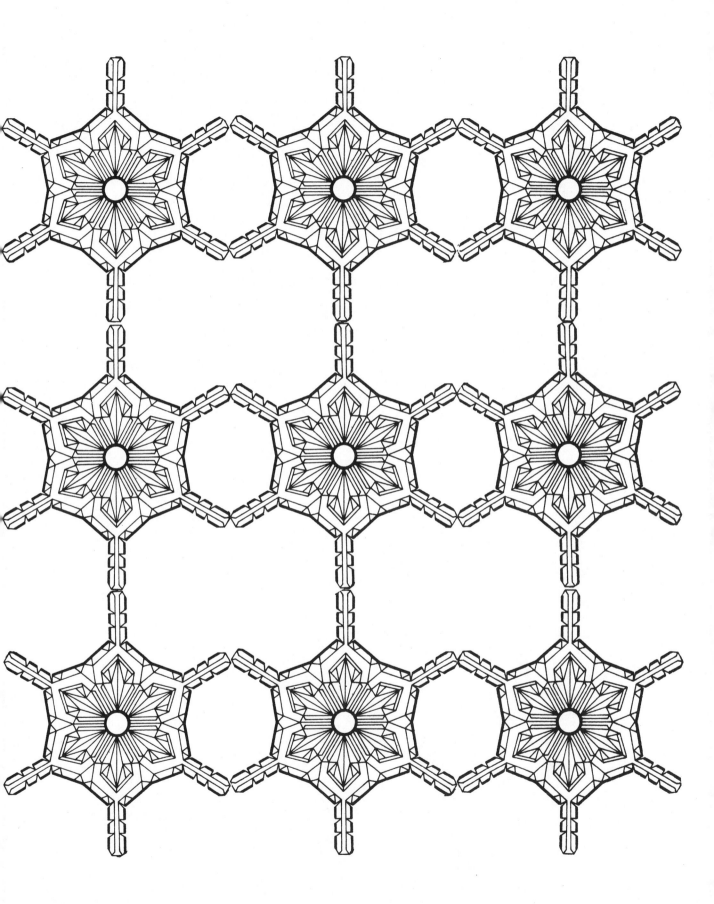